Salads & Dressings

DAVID & CHARLES
Newton Abbot London

British Library Cataloguing in Publication Data

Salads and Dressings.—(David & Charles Kitchen Workshop)
  1. Salads
  I. Salater. *English*
  641.8′3   TX807

  ISBN 0-7153-8454-6

© Illustrations: A/S Hjemmet 1981
Text: David & Charles 1983

Filmset by MS Filmsetting Ltd, Frome, Somerset
and printed in The Netherlands
by Smeets Offset BV, Weert
for David & Charles (Publishers) Limited
Brunel House Newton Abbot Devon

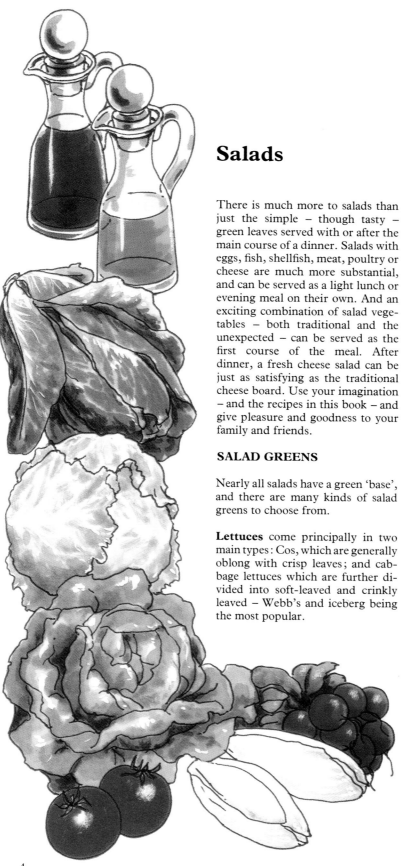

Salads

There is much more to salads than just the simple – though tasty – green leaves served with or after the main course of a dinner. Salads with eggs, fish, shellfish, meat, poultry or cheese are much more substantial, and can be served as a light lunch or evening meal on their own. And an exciting combination of salad vegetables – both traditional and the unexpected – can be served as the first course of the meal. After dinner, a fresh cheese salad can be just as satisfying as the traditional cheese board. Use your imagination – and the recipes in this book – and give pleasure and goodness to your family and friends.

SALAD GREENS

Nearly all salads have a green 'base', and there are many kinds of salad greens to choose from.

Lettuces come principally in two main types: Cos, which are generally oblong with crisp leaves; and cabbage lettuces which are further divided into soft-leaved and crinkly leaved – Webb's and iceberg being the most popular.

Always choose lettuces with fresh and bright leaves, and avoid those which look or feel slimy or have brown patches on the outer leaves. Divide the leaves of Cos lettuce, wash and dry carefully, and then cut or tear to desired size; do the same with Webb's, but iceberg – increasingly popular and available in Britain, although expensive – can be shredded or cut like a cabbage. These crisp lettuces will keep for at least a week in a plastic bag in the refrigerator.

Chinese cabbage is oblong in shape, like Cos lettuce, with crisp, slightly curly leaves. This type of lettuce has become more popular recently, because it is both tasty and keeps well. You can wash Chinese cabbage, slice it and leave it in a plastic bag in the refrigerator for 8–10 days. Even when dressed, a Chinese cabbage will stay crisp for a while.

Spinach. Fresh spinach is an excellent salad green, but it bruises easily, so must be handled carefully. It also wilts quickly, so buy when the leaves are crisp to the touch, and use it straightaway. Spinach is full of nutritional goodness.

Watercress is well suited to salads. Avoid bunches that are in flower, or have a high proportion of yellow or wilting leaves. Watercress, like spinach, has a high vitamin and mineral content.

Endive is a salad green similar to lettuce, with curly, crisp leaves, and a slightly bitter flavour. Choose firm dry endive, avoiding those which look slimy at the base. Do not confuse with Belgian endive which is known as chicory in the UK.

Raw grated carrot, small marrows or courgettes, and kohlrabi (or swede or turnip) are tasty alternatives for a salad based on greens.

MORE SALAD VEGETABLES

Beansprouts add a good flavour to various kinds of salads. You can buy them in tins, but they are better loose and fresh, and you can even grow them yourself (the sprouts of Adzuki or Mung beans).

Chicory has a conical white head of crisp leaves packed firmly together. Avoid any with yellow curling leaves. Chicory is crisp in texture with a slightly bitter taste, and is excellent for winter salads, or mixed with salad greens of all kinds.

Fennel, or Florence fennel, to differentiate it from the herb, is now comparatively widely available, and has a distinct aniseed flavour. It adds a crisp crunch not unlike celery to a salad, and keeps about 1 week in the refrigerator.

Celery can be creamy white or light green. Choose thick celery heads, plump at the base, with smooth stalks, and healthy looking leaves, if any, which indicate freshness. Pull any tough threads or strings from individual stalks. It keeps in a plastic bag in the fridge for about 1 week.

Celeriac is a turnip-rooted form of celery, and its taste is very similar. It is a winter vegetable, becoming more popular in Britain, and may be replaced by celery in any recipe if difficult to obtain.

In general, though, almost all vegetables can be used in salads – and we haven't even mentioned the salad basics of tomatoes, spring onions, cucumber, radishes or mustard and cress ...

5

Salad Sauces

Salad sauces are those which contain mayonnaise, eggs, sour cream, butter, yoghurt, cottage cheese or cream cheese as a base – used instead of oil, which makes a 'salad dressing'. Sauces are thinned out to a suitable consistency with lemon juice, wine vinegar, wine or other ingredients, and are seasoned according to the type of salad and flavour required. Fresh herbs and onions are often added.

Salad sauces should be left to settle for a few minutes before tasting and finally seasoning. They should be eaten straightaway. They do not store in the refrigerator, nor can they be frozen.

Homemade Mayonnaise

2 egg-yolks
1 × 15ml tbsp (1tbsp) lemon juice
1 × 5ml tsp (1tsp) salt
about 300ml (½pt) olive oil

Whisk egg-yolks until light and fluffy with ½ the lemon juice and the salt. Add oil drop by drop to start with and then in a thin stream, whisking or stirring vigorously and continuously.

The mayonnaise should look constantly smooth and shiny. If it shows signs of curdling, whisk in 1–2 × 5ml tsp (1–2tsp) ice-cold water or a small ice-cube. Season the mayonnaise with more lemon juice and sprinkle with white pepper.

NB: All ingredients, the bowl and whisks, must be at the same temperature, and not too cold. Leave everything you are going to use out for a couple of hours in advance, to allow it all to come to room temperature.

Blender Mayonnaise

1 whole egg
2 egg-yolks
½ × 5ml tsp (½tsp) salt
2 × 5ml tsp (2tsp) white wine
*   vinegar or lemon juice*
250ml (9fl oz) olive oil

Break the egg into the blender goblet and add egg-yolks, salt, wine vinegar or lemon juice, and ½ the oil. Blend for 30 secs at medium speed. Pour the remaining oil in a thin stream through the hole in the lid, with the blender still on, for about 1 min or until the mayonnaise is mixed. Season with salt and lemon juice or wine vinegar.

Green Salad Sauce

2 shallots or small onions
5–6 Chinese cabbage or iceberg
*   lettuce leaves*
3 × 15ml tbsp (3tbsp) olive oil
200ml (7fl oz) sour cream
1 × 15ml tbsp (1tbsp) lemon juice
1 sprig of parsley
2 × 15ml tbsp (2tbsp) finely chopped
*   chives or cress*
salt, white pepper

Finely chop the onions. Wash and coarsely chop the leaves. Sauté both lightly in oil until onion is soft. Put in the blender goblet along with the other ingredients and blend at medium speed until sauce is smooth. The mixture can also be pressed through a fine-mesh sieve and the other ingredients whisked in.

Leave sauce in a cold place for ½ hr and season with salt and pepper. This green sauce is suitable for salads to accompany ham, poultry, sausages and fried meat.

Yoghurt and Herb Sauce

about 200ml (7fl oz) plain yoghurt
2 × 15ml tbsp (2tbsp) lemon juice
2 × 15ml tbsp (2tbsp) olive oil
1 shallot or small onion
2–3 × 15ml tbsp (2tbsp) finely
*   chopped herbs (see method)*
salt, white pepper

Whisk yoghurt with lemon juice and oil. Add grated or very finely chopped onions and herbs – chives, parsley, dill, cress or watercress.
This sauce goes well with salads made from raw vegetables.

Mustard Salad Sauce

1 × 15ml tbsp (1tbsp) strong made
*   mustard*
1 × 15ml tbsp (1tbsp) white wine
*   vinegar*
1 × 15ml tbsp (1tbsp) water
3 × 15ml tbsp (3tbsp) olive oil
1 egg-yolk
1 hard-boiled egg
1 × 15ml tbsp (1tbsp) finely chopped
*   cress*
salt, pepper

Whisk mustard, vinegar and water with oil to a creamy consistency and whisk in the raw egg-yolk. Add finely chopped, hard-boiled eggs and cress. Season with salt and pepper.
This sauce goes best with salads accompanying ham, bacon or pork.

Walnut Salad Sauce

100g (4oz) mayonnaise
100ml (4fl oz) plain yoghurt
100ml (4fl oz) sour cream
1 × 15ml tbsp (1tbsp) lemon juice
a pinch of curry powder
1 × 5ml tsp (1tsp) mustard
50g (2oz) walnuts, finely chopped
salt, pepper

Mix mayonnaise with yoghurt, sour cream and lemon juice. Add curry powder, mustard and finely chopped walnuts. Leave sauce to settle for about ½ hr before seasoning with a pinch of salt and pepper. Serve with raw vegetable salads, with crudités, and salads with chicken or ham.

Tangy salad dressings make any
salad taste even better.

Dressings

The most commonly used – and tastiest – salad dressing is the French dressing or vinaigrette mix-ture of oil and vinegar.

As a rule the proportions are 1 part wine vinegar to 3 parts oil, but this always depends on the flavour re-quired and your own preference. Many like to mix an equal propor-tion of oil and vinegar. The vinegar can also be replaced by lemon juice or, even better, white wine. Spices, herbs and other flavourings are wide in choice. Dressings are not suitable for the freezer.

Salad sauces should be used within a day or two, while dressings can be stored in the fridge for a couple of weeks.

Basic French Dressing

Stir 1 part wine vinegar or spiced vinegar well with salt, pepper and dry mustard. Whisk, stir or shake in about 3 parts good quality fresh oil. The oil can be more neutral in flavour – like corn, soy or sunflower – or it can add its own special flavour to the dressing – like olive oil or walnut oil, for instance.

This basic dressing can be made in large quantities and kept in bottles with screw-tops. It will keep well for about 1 week in the refrigerator. Pour out what you need each day to dress salads, and spice it well with onion, garlic, herbs, wine, mustard, curry, paprika or other flavourings.

Red Wine Dressing

2 shallots or small onions
2 pickled gherkins
1 × 15ml tbsp (1tbsp) small capers
2 × 15ml tbsp (2 tbsp) red wine vinegar
1 × 15ml tbsp (1tbsp) tomato purée
5–6 × 15ml tbsp (5–6tbsp) oil
salt, black pepper

Finely chop the onions and pickled gherkins and mix with capers and the other ingredients. Add salt and pepper to taste. Allow dressing to settle before pouring over the salad. Use on salad to accompany beef.

French Herb Dressing

2–3 × 15ml tbsp (2–3tbsp) white wine vinegar
150ml (¼pt) olive oil
4–5 stems of basil and/or marjoram, rosemary
1 clove of garlic
salt, white pepper

Mix vinegar and oil in a small glass jar. Add sticks of fresh, washed herbs, crushed garlic and salt and pepper to taste. Allow dressing to settle for at least 2 hrs before sprinkling over green salads.

This dressing will keep for about 1 week in fridge.

Garlic Dressing

2 garlic cloves
½ × 5ml tsp (½tsp) salt
1 × 15ml tbsp (1tbsp) finely chopped chives
1 spring onion with green top or 1 thin leek
2 × 15ml tbsp (2tbsp) white wine vinegar
5–6 × 15ml tbsp (5–6tbsp) oil
black pepper

Coarsely chop the garlic cloves on a bread board, sprinkle with salt and crush garlic with a wooden spoon or a soft knife. Put garlic in a bowl and add finely chopped chives, finely chopped onion or finely shredded leek. Mix vinegar and oil together and mix with vegetables. Season with salt and pepper.

This dressing is suitable for all green salads to be served with beef, veal or lamb.

From the left: Garlic Dressing, Herb Dressing, Red Wine Dressing, and Port Dressing.

Herb Dressing

2 × 15ml tbsp (2tbsp) tarragon vinegar
1–2 onions
1 sprig of parsley
1 sprig fresh tarragon or 2 × 5ml tsp (2tsp) dried
1 × 15ml tbsp (1tbsp) finely chopped chives
5–6 × 15ml tbsp (5–6tbsp) oil
salt, black pepper

Mix vinegar with finely chopped onion, finely chopped parsley, tarragon and chives and whisk oil into dressing. Season with salt and pepper.

Pour dressing over a green or raw vegetable salad.

Port Dressing

1 red pepper
1 hard-boiled egg
2 × 15ml tbsp (2tbsp) finely chopped dill
2–3 × 15ml tbsp (2–3tbsp) port
3 × 15ml tbsp (3tbsp) lemon juice
4–5 × 15ml tbsp (4–5tbsp) oil
salt, pepper

Wash, peel, deseed and finely chop pepper. Mix with coarsely chopped egg and other ingredients. Allow dressing to settle in a cold place before seasoning with salt and pepper. This dressing goes well with green salads to accompany fish or shellfish.

Salads to Suit Everyone

Tuna Fish Salad
(serves 4–6)
Preparation time: about 15 min

1 green pepper
2–3 shallots or small onions
4 ripe tomatoes
1–2 cans tuna fish
10–12 stuffed olives
a few lettuce leaves
Pink Salad Sauce (see page 32)

1 Wash and dry pepper, halve lengthwise and take out the seeds. Slice into narrow strips. Slice onions into small rings and the tomatoes into wedges.
2 Flake well-drained tuna, slice olives, and rinse lettuce leaves.
3 Place lettuce leaves in individual glasses, mix the other ingredients and divide between glasses. Place a spoonful of salad sauce on top of each portion.
Serve freshly made with rolls or crisp French bread.

Shrimp Salad
(serves 4)
Preparation time: 10–20 min

1 can asparagus (about 250g or 9oz)
about ½kg (1¼lb) fresh or frozen shrimps or 200g (7oz) peeled, tinned ones
1 lettuce
1 sprig of dill
½ lemon
Pink Salad Sauce (see page 32)

1 Drain asparagus thoroughly.
2 Defrost frozen shrimps by pouring into boiling salted water with some dill. Remove saucepan from heat and allow shrimps to cool in stock. Peel them.
3 Place shredded lettuce at the bottom of individual glasses and sprinkle a touch of lemon juice on top. Mix asparagus and shrimps in sauce and divide between glasses. Garnish with a few extra shrimps and asparagus tips and dill.
Serve with melba toast.

Juicy Tuna Fish Salad with fluffy Pink Salad Sauce makes a good starter or a complete meal when served with French bread and butter.

Salmon Salad
(serves 6)
Preparation time: about 20 min

3 eggs
1 lettuce
1 can asparagus
175–200g (6–7oz) cold, poached salmon (or canned)
100g (4oz) mayonnaise
1–2 lemons
salt, pepper
1 small jar Danish caviar (lumpfish roe)
dill

1 Hard-boiled eggs, remove shells and halve. Rinse lettuce and shake off excess water.
2 Place whole lettuce leaves or shredded lettuce on small plates and arrange egg wedges, asparagus and well-drained salmon chunks on top.
3 Mix mayonnaise with juice of ½–1 lemon and blend in caviar carefully. Season sauce with salt and pepper and pour over salad.
Garnish with fresh dill and lemon wedges, and serve with toast.

Crab Salad
(serves 4)
Preparation time: about 20 min

1 can crab meat (about 175–200g or 6–7oz)
1 avocado pear
1 lemon
salt, white pepper
100g (4oz) mushrooms
50g (2oz) small green peas, lightly steamed
Green Salad Sauce (see page 6)

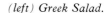
(left) Greek Salad.

1 Drain crab meat and remove any bits of shell. Halve avocado, remove stone, and peel. Cut flesh into small cubes, and sprinkle with salt and pepper. Squeeze the juice of the lemon over the avocado cubes.

2 Clean mushrooms and slice. Mix avocado cubes with mushrooms and mix this and most of the crabmeat into the salad sauce.

3 Divide the salad between 4 glasses and place peas and remaining crab on top.

Serve with toasted brown bread and butter.

Californian Salad
(serves 4–6)
Preparation time: 15–20 min

1 lettuce, 1 grapefruit
1 small fresh pineapple or 1 can
*   unsweetened, sliced pineapple*
about 200g (7oz) mushrooms
4–6 small tomatoes
200g (7oz) peeled shrimps
4–5 × 15ml tbsp (4–5tbsp)
*   mayonnaise*
1 lemon
salt, pepper

1 Rinse lettuce leaves and shake dry in a cloth. Place on a large, flat dish. Halve grapefruit and remove flesh with a grapefruit knife or a pointed, sharp spoon. Keep the juice for use in the sauce.

2 Cut the fresh pineapple in four, lengthways, after cutting off the top. Peel it, remove the central core, and slice flesh into small pieces. Use canned pineapple as it is, but well drained. Cut peeled, cleaned mushrooms into slices and tomatoes into wedges.

3 Mix all these ingredients lightly together with the shrimps, and place on top of lettuce leaves.

4 Mix together a sauce of mayonnaise, the grapefruit juice, lemon juice, and salt and pepper. Serve freshly made with dressing, and rolls or toast with butter.

Californian Salad is an exciting combination of fresh fruit and shrimps.

Greek Salad

(serves 4)
Preparation time: about 15 min

1 lettuce
1 bunch of radishes
4 small tomatoes
1 small white turnip
15–20 stoneless, black olives
100–150g (4–5oz) Feta cheese, or
fresh cream or cottage cheese
200ml (7fl oz) buttermilk or sour
cream
lemon juice
salt, pepper
2 × 15ml tbsp (2tbsp) finely chopped
herbs (see method)

1 Rinse the lettuce and shake dry in a cloth. Place leaves on small plates or on a large, flat dish. Cut turnip and radishes into thin slices.
2 Cut tomatoes into wedges, coarsely chop the olives and break cheese into pieces. Place all ingredients nicely on top of lettuce leaves.

3 Mix together a salad sauce of buttermilk or sour cream, season with lemon juice, salt, pepper and finely chopped herbs (eg, chives, cress, parsley or dill). Pour some over the salad, and serve the rest separately. Serve salad freshly made, with Greek pitta bread or ordinary bread.

Kohlrabi or Turnip Salad

(serves 6)
Preparation time: about 20 min

6 small kohlrabi or turnips
1 lemon
salt, pepper
celery salt (optional)
1 red and 1 green pepper
300ml (½pt) plain yoghurt
paprika
chili sauce or Tabasco

1 Wash and peel kohlrabi or turnips. Allow some of the nicest small leaves to remain and cut off a lid.

Kohlrabi's nutty, turnip-like flavour makes it a Continental favourite. It deserves to be more widely available here as it matures in only 10–12 weeks from sowing, withstands frost, and stores well.

Carve them out with a grapefruit knife or some other sharp knife and cut the flesh into small cubes. Turn immediately in lemon juice and sprinkle with a touch of salt and pepper or other spices to taste.
2 Wash and deseed peppers and cut into cubes.
3 Mix together a dressing of yoghurt, well seasoned with chili sauce or Tabasco, paprika and a pinch of salt. Mix kohlrabi or turnip and pepper cubes together in the dressing and leave in a cold place for 15–20 min.
Fill the carved-out kohlrabi or turnips with the salad.

13

Salads from Abroad

Americans are the best at making salads. The French have their specialities and around the Mediterranean they make delicious shellfish salads. Be adventurous.

Luxury Seafood Salad

(serves 6)
Preparation time: 15–20 min

6 ripe tomatoes
1 lettuce
about 200g (7oz) green beans
1 can artichoke bottoms
1 can crab or mussels
50–100g (2–4oz) smoked salmon
4 small pickled gherkins
3 × 15ml tbsp (3tbsp) lemon juice
1 garlic clove
salt, pepper
2 × 15ml tbsp (2tbsp) finely chopped parsley
4–5 × 15ml tbsp (4–5tbsp) olive oil

1 Scald and skin tomatoes, and cut into quarters. Rinse lettuce leaves, shake off excess water and shred. Boil beans until just tender in lightly salted water and drain in a colander.
2 Drain juices from artichokes and crabs or mussels and cut artichoke hearts into pieces. Remove any bone from crab meat. Cube salmon and gherkins.
3 Mix all ingredients in a salad bowl. Shake together a dressing of lemon juice, crushed garlic, salt, pepper, parsley and oil, and sprinkle over salad.
Serve freshly made with toast or white bread and butter.

Left: Filling Luxury Seafood Salad can be served as a main course.

Right: In Spain and around the Mediterranean shellfish and chicken are often served together as in this Mediterranean Salad.

Mediterranean Salad

(serves 4)
Preparation time: about 20 min

1 lettuce
4 tomatoes
1 can tuna fish
1 can artichoke hearts or bottoms
200g (7oz) peeled shrimps
10–12 stuffed olives
left-over cold chicken (optional)
4–5 × 15ml tbsp (4–5tbsp) mayonnaise
lemon juice
2 × 15ml tbsp (2tbsp) tomato purée
salt, pepper, paprika
fresh dill

1 Wash and dry crisp lettuce leaves and place at the bottom and slightly up the sides of a lettuce bowl. Scald and skin tomatoes, and cut into quarters.
2 Cut drained tuna and artichoke into small pieces, and olives and chicken (if used) into thin, fine slices. Mix all ingredients together and place in bowl on top of lettuce.
3 Season mayonnaise with lemon juice, tomato purée and spices. Pour over salad and sprinkle with finely chopped dill. Garnish with a couple of sprigs of dill on top. Serve with French bread, rolls or thin slices of toast.

Belgian Cheese Salad

(serves 4)
Preparation time: about 15 min

about 200g (7oz) cottage cheese
2 eggs, salt, pepper
1 × 15ml tbsp (1 tbsp) white wine
  vinegar
1 bunch of chives
25–50g (1–2oz) chopped walnuts
1 thin leek
4 small tomatoes
¼ cucumber

1 Hard-boil the eggs, remove the shells and coarsely chop them. Mix cottage cheese with wine vinegar, salt and pepper to taste. Fold in chopped eggs carefully, and then finely chopped chives and walnuts.
2 Peel and slice leek into thin rings, tomatoes into wedges and cucumber into cubes. Sprinkle a pinch of salt over tomatoes and cucumbers.
3 Place tomatoes, cucumber and leek rings in piles round a dish and place the cheese mixture in the middle.
Serve with toast or small salty biscuits.

Greek Mushroom Salad

(serves 4–6)
Preparation time: about 15 min
Marination time: 1–2 hrs

250g (9oz) small shallots or button
  onions
½kg (1¼lb) fresh button mushrooms
2 bay leaves
1 sprig of thyme
2 lemons
salt, pepper
about 300–400ml (½–¾pt) olive oil

1 Place onions in a sieve, pour boiling water over and rinse as quickly as possible in cold water. Peel onions. Bring lightly salted water to the boil, and add bay leaves and thyme. Place onions in water and allow to boil for 5 min. Drain.
2 Clean mushrooms, rinse separately under cold, running water and drain in a sieve or colander.
3 Mix warm onions and whole mushrooms in a salad bowl. Shake together a dressing of lemon juice, salt, pepper and olive oil and pour over salad. Place bay leaves and thyme in bowl too, and leave under cover in a cold place for 1–2 hrs.
Serve salad cold with brown bread.

Watercress and Egg Salad – a French favourite.

Watercress and Egg Salad

(serves 4)
Preparation time: about 15 min

1 large bunch watercress
3 eggs
salt, pepper
2 × 15ml tbsp (2 tbsp) white wine
  vinegar
5–6 × 15ml tbsp (5–6tbsp) oil

1 Rinse cress well and shake off all excess water. Remove the thickest stalks. Hard-boil the eggs and remove shells.

2 Chop up 2 of the eggs and sprinkle them with a dressing of vinegar, salt, pepper and oil. Mix with the watercress and garnish with slices of the third egg. Serve salad with French bread.

VARIATION
If preferred, finely chopped lettuce, chicory or Chinese cabbage may be substituted for the watercress.

Breton Salad

(serves 4)
Preparation time: 10–15 min

1 can artichoke bottoms
1 can mussels (about 200g or 7oz)
4 ripe tomatoes
3 celery stalks
2 hard-boiled eggs
200 ml (7fl oz) sour cream
1 sprig of dill
2 lemons, salt and pepper

1 Drain brine from artichokes and mussels, and slice artichokes into strips. Cut tomatoes into wedges and the celery stalks into thin, narrow strips. Halve the eggs, remove yolks and coarsely chop the whites.
2 Mix together a salad sauce of sour cream and lemon juice, add egg whites and finely chopped dill. Season with salt and pepper.
3 Place celery strips on a flat dish and place artichokes, mussels and tomatoes in stripes on top. Cut lemon into wedges and place along the edge. Sieve the hard-boiled yolks over the salad. Place some of the salad sauce in a stripe across the salad and serve the rest separately. Serve with French bread.

Greek Cucumber Salad

(serves 4–5)
Preparation time: about 10 min
Settling time: about 30 min

1 cucumber
salt, 1 lemon
200–300ml (7–10fl oz) plain
  yoghurt
1 onion, 1–2 cloves of garlic
pepper
2 × 15ml tbsp (2tbsp) finely chopped
  chives

1 Wash cucumber, slice into small cubes and sprinkle with a touch of coarse salt. Place cubes in a colander, weight down lightly, and leave for 15–20 min.
2 Mix together a dressing of yoghurt, lemon juice, grated onion, crushed garlic, finely chopped chives, a pinch of salt and pepper to taste.
3 Shake cucumber cubes dry in a cloth and mix into the salad sauce. Leave salad in a cold place for 10–15 min.
Serve with lamb or beef dishes.

Tomato and Olive Salad with Feta cheese.

Tomato and Olive Salad

(serves 4)
Preparation time: about 10 min
Settling time: about 30 min

4–6 ripe tomatoes
¼ cucumber
100g (4oz) black olives
100g (4oz) Feta or cottage cheese
1 lemon, salt, pepper
50–75ml (2–3fl oz) olive oil
fresh or dried basil

1 Rinse and dry tomatoes and cu-
cumber. Slice. Place cucumber and tomato slices in overlapping circles on a plate or dish and sprinkle with a pinch of salt (see photograph above).
2 Place olives and small pieces of Feta or cottage cheese over cucumber and tomatoes, and dress with a little lemon juice.
3 Rinse fresh basil well, chop leaves into strips and sprinkle over salad. If you use dried basil, crumble it and mix with oil. Sprinkle salad with oil and leave in a cold place.
Serve with brown bread.

Creole Salad

(serves 5–6)
Preparation time: about 15 min

100–200g (4–7oz) small shallots or
    button onions
salt
200g (7oz) green beans
1 × 5ml tsp (1tsp) tarragon vinegar
2 cooked corn on the cobs or 225g
    (½lb) sweetcorn (frozen or
    canned)
2 slices of white bread, crusts
    removed
oil
1 clove garlic
6 small tomatoes
2 × 15ml tbsp (2tbsp) red wine
    vinegar
black pepper
paprika
fresh herbs

1 Blanch onion for a minute in boiling water, then peel and place in boiling, lightly salted water with the prepared beans. Add tarragon vinegar and boil vegetables for 4–5 min. Drain vegetables in a sieve or colander and leave to cool.

2 Scrape corns off the cobs and cool. If using frozen corn, add to the saucepan with onion and beans and allow to boil for 1 min before other vegetables are ready.

3 Cut bread slices into cubes, and

sauté in oil with crushed garlic. Drain on paper towels.

4 Mix onions, beans, sweet corn and bread cubes with tomatoes cut into thin wedges. Sprinkle with a dressing of vinegar, salt, pepper paprika, 5–6 × 15ml tbsp (5–6tbsp) oil and 2–3 × 15ml tbsp (2–3tbsp) finely chopped herbs (chives, cress, parsley or basil).

Serve salad with lamb or poultry.

Portuguese Ham Salad is a wonderful mixture of tastes and textures.

Dijon Celeriac Salad

(serves 4)
Preparation time: about 15 min
Settling time: about 30 min

¼–½ celeriac
1 × 15ml tbsp (1tbsp) tarragon
   vinegar
2 × 15ml tbsp (2tbsp) mayonnaise
about 100ml (4fl oz) sour cream
1–2 × 15ml tbsp (1–2tbsp) Dijon
   mustard
salt
white pepper
parsley

1 Peel celeriac and grate coarsely into a bowl with a little water and a few ice-cubes. Sprinkle tarragon vinegar on top and leave for 10–15 min.
2 Mix the mayonnaise and sour cream together, and season well with mustard. Leave sauce for 10 min and season with salt and pepper.
3 Drain celeriac in a colander thoroughly (squeeze the strips). Mix into the sauce and sprinkle with parsley.
Serve with chicken and boiled ham.

Portuguese Ham Salad

(serves 4–5)
Preparation time: about 15 min

2–3 slices of white bread, crusts
   removed
1 clove garlic
oil
1 lettuce
2 thick slices ham
4–6 tomatoes
2 thin spring onions or 1 bunch of
   chives
50g (2oz) small black olives
1 small can anchovy fillets
100g (4oz) Feta or cottage cheese
2–3 × 15ml tbsp (2–3tbsp) white
   wine vinegar
6–8 × 15ml tbsp (6–8tbsp) olive oil
salt, pepper
parsley

1 Cut bread into cubes and sauté until lightly brown in oil with crushed garlic. Drain bread cubes on paper towels.
2 Rinse outer lettuce leaves and shake off excess water. Cut ham into cubes, wash tomatoes and cut into four wedges. Chop onions or finely chop chives.
3 Cut lettuce heart into rough strips

and mix with fried bread cubes, ham, tomatoes, onion, olives and well-drained anchovy fillets. Add roughly torn outer lettuce leaves and small pieces of cheese on top.
4 Shake together a dressing of wine vinegar, salt, pepper and olive oil or other good oil. Pour dressing over salad and sprinkle with finely chopped parsley.
Serve salad with brown bread.

Caesar Salad

(serves 4–5)
Preparation time: about 15 min

1 Chinese cabbage or crisp Cos
   lettuce
2–3 slices of white bread, crusts
   removed
1 clove of garlic
oil
3–4 anchovy fillets
1 egg
1 × 15ml tbsp (1tbsp) red wine
   vinegar
1 × 15ml tbsp (1tbsp) lemon juice
salt, pepper
3 × 15ml tbsp (3tbsp) grated
   Parmesan cheese

1 Rinse Chinese cabbage leaves separately and shake in a cloth until dry. Cut or tear leaves into fairly big pieces and place in a salad bowl, which has been rubbed with half a garlic clove.
2 Cut bread into cubes and sauté until lightly golden and crisp in oil mixed with the remaining ½ garlic clove, crushed. Drain bread cubes on paper towels.
3 Drain the anchovy fillets thoroughly and chop them finely. Boil egg for 1 min and place in cold water immediately.
4 Mix together a dressing of red wine vinegar, lemon juice, salt, pepper and 3–4 × 15ml tbsp (3–4tbsp) oil. Scrape the nearly raw egg out of the shell into the dressing. Whisk egg well into the dressing.
5 Prepare the salad bowl, croûtons, dressing and the grated cheese in advance, and mix salad just before serving.
Add dressing and grated cheese alternatively to the bowl, in small amounts, turning the cabbage or lettuce leaves all the time. The cheese soaks up the dressing and leaves the lettuce crisp. Finally, sprinkle the croûtons on top, and serve at once.

Green Spring Salad

(serves 4)
Preparation time: 15–20 min

about 350g (¾lb) green beans
½ cauliflower
½ cucumber
about 200g (7oz) fresh or frozen
  peas
about 200g (7oz) fresh spinach or 1
  small lettuce
200ml (7fl oz) plain yoghurt
lemon juice
salt, pepper
finely chopped green herbs

1 Clean all vegetables, boil beans until barely tender in lightly salted water and divide cauliflower into small florets. Slice cucumber, and sprinkle with a pinch of salt.
2 Thaw frozen peas and rinse and drain spinach or lettuce leaves. Place all vegetables in a bowl or in small piles on a serving platter.
3 Mix together yoghurt and lemon juice, season with salt and pepper and mix in about 2 × 15ml tbsp (2tbsp) finely chopped green herbs. Pour some of the sauce over the salad and serve the rest separately. Serve freshly made with brown bread.

Mushroom Salad

(serves 6)
Preparation time: about 20 min

1 medium Chinese cabbage
350–450g (¾–1lb) fresh mushrooms
1–2 lemons
salt, pepper
about 300ml (½pt) sour cream
25–50g (1–2oz) shelled walnuts

1 Rinse Chinese cabbage and shred. Shake until completely dry in a cloth and place in the refrigerator in a plastic bag until you need it (this keeps it crisp).
2 Remove some of the stalks from the mushrooms and rinse them separately under cold, running water. Drain in a colander.
3 Squeeze juice of 1 large or 2 small lemons into a bowl. Slice the mushroom into the lemon juice and turn to avoid discolouring.
Mix sour cream carefully with mushrooms and lemon juice and mix in the cabbage shreds. Season with salt and pepper and garnish with whole or chopped walnuts.

Vegetable Platter is a good – and healthy – start to any meal.

Mexican Pepper Salad

(serves 4–5)
Preparation time: about 15 min
Settling time: about 1 hr

1 yellow and 1 green pepper
4–6 ripe tomatoes
175–250g (6–9oz) cooked haricot
  beans
200ml (7fl oz) buttermilk or
  skimmed milk
chili sauce to taste
1 onion
1 garlic clove
salt, pepper
paprika
finely chopped chives

1 Wash and deseed peppers, and cut into small cubes. Place in a plastic bag in the fridge while preparing the rest of the salad.
2 Mix buttermilk or skimmed milk with chili sauce to taste. Add grated or finely chopped onion and crushed garlic. Mix in boiled, cold beans and leave mixture covered in a cold place for 1 hr before seasoning.
3 Cut tomatoes into slices and place along the edge of small serving plates. Mix pepper cubes into the salad sauce with beans and divide between the plates.
Sprinkle with chives and serve with brown bread.

Serve well chilled with rolls as a first course or as a main course with meat or fish.

Vegetable Platter
(serves 4)
Preparation time: about 15 min

2 carrots
2 small heads of chicory
1 thin leek
200ml (7fl oz) plain yoghurt
½ lemon
salt, pepper
dill, chervil
cress
lemon balm (or mint)

1 Peel vegetables. Coarsely grate carrots. Cut away some of the root on the chicory with a sharp knife. Cut leek and chicory into thin strips.
2 Mix yoghurt with lemon juice, salt, pepper and a generous handful of finely chopped herbs. Place the vegetables on plates, pour a spoonful of salad sauce over and garnish with cress.
Serve freshly made, with bread and a slice of ham or other cold meat.

Rainbow Salad
(serves 4–5)
Preparation time: about 15 min

6–8 small, ripe tomatoes
6–8 spring onions with green or 2 thin leeks
about 200g (7oz) sweetcorn (frozen or canned)
½ cucumber
2–3 carrots
1 lemon
3 × 15ml tbsp (3tbsp) oil
mustard
salt, pepper

1 Clean and prepare all vegetables. Cut tomatoes into narrow wedges and onions or leeks into thin rings.
2 Defrost frozen corn or rinse canned corn in cold water, and drain in a colander. Cut cucumber into cubes and coarsely grate scraped carrots.
3 Place all ingredients in a rainbow pattern on a flat dish and sprinkle with a dressing of lemon juice, oil, mustard, salt and pepper.
Serve salad well chilled as an accompaniment to fried meat or poultry.

Lunch or dinner on a hot day – a cool, tasty Portuguese Salad.

Portuguese Salad
(serves 4)
Preparation time: about 15 min

1 can of sardines (skinned and boned)
3–4 boiled potatoes
3 hard-boiled eggs
6 slices cooked or pickled beetroot
3 pickled gherkins or a chunk of cucumber
1 can of anchovy fillets
2 × 15ml tbsp (2tbsp) red wine vinegar
salt, pepper
oil
lettuce
fresh spinach leaves or fresh cress

1 Place pieces of well drained sardines in groups on plates. Cut cold, boiled potatoes into small cubes and the eggs into wedges and place next to the sardines.
2 Coarsely chop beetroot and cucumber or gherkins, and place on plates with the well drained anchovy fillets.
Mix a dressing of wine vinegar, salt, pepper and oil to taste and sprinkle over the salad. Garnish each plate with fresh, rinsed lettuce leaves, spinach or cress.
Serve freshly made with brown bread.

Salads with Fish and Shellfish

Cod Roe Salad
(serves 4)
Preparation time: about 15 min
Settling time: about 20 min

about 200g (7oz) boiled cod roe
2 lemons
2 eggs
about 300ml (½pt) sour cream
salt, pepper
paprika
1 green pepper
a few lettuce leaves
stuffed olives
fresh dill

1 Remove skin from roe and mash with a fork. Sprinkle with juice of ½ lemon.
2 Hard-boil eggs and remove shells.

Make a salad sauce with sour cream and juice of ½ lemon. Chop one egg finely and mix into salad sauce.
3 Clean and deseed pepper and cut into fairly small cubes. Mix roe and pepper cubes into sauce, and season. Allow salad to stand in a cool place for about 20 min.
4 Rinse lettuce leaves and spread on a dish. Place cod roe salad on leaves and garnish with wedges of egg and lemon, olives, and sprigs of dill. Serve salad with toast.

Sunday Salad
(serves 6)
Preparation time: about 10 min

1 large lettuce
1 can asparagus chunks
1 can mussels
200–400g (7–14oz) peeled shrimps
2–3 eggs
fresh dill
½ portion Walnut Salad Sauce (see page 6)

If using frozen shrimps, defrost in a saucepan with boiling salted water with a couple of sprigs of dill. (The shrimps should not be allowed to boil, just put in the boiling water and leave to cool.)
1 Rinse lettuce leaves and dry well. Drain mussels, asparagus and shrimps thoroughly.
2 Hard-boil the eggs, rinse in cold water, and shell. Cut eggs into wedges and mix with the other ingredients in a salad bowl.
Garnish with small sprigs of dill and some of the salad sauce. Serve with warm rolls, French bread or toast and the remaining salad sauce.

Carnival Salad
(serves 4–6)
Preparation time: 15–20 min

1 green and 1 red pepper
2 eggs
1 small lettuce
1 orange or grapefruit
8–12 large mushrooms
10–12 stuffed olives
100–200g (4–7oz) peeled shrimps
1 can mussels
½ lemon
1 portion Green Salad Sauce (page 6)

1 Wash and dry peppers, remove seeds, and cut flesh into strips. Hard-boil the eggs, remove shell and slice into wedges.
2 Rinse and dry lettuce leaves. Peel orange or grapefruit, remove all membranes and slice flesh into small chunks. Clean mushrooms, slice, and sprinkle with lemon juice. Slice olives.
3 Pour mussels into a sieve and leave to drain well. Mix all ingredients in a dish or a bowl and pour salad sauce over.

Sunday Salad.

Colourful Carnival Salad.

West Coast Salad
(serves 4–6)
Preparation time: 10–15 min

100–200g (4–7oz) green beans
¼ cucumber
2–3 eggs
4 tomatoes
½ green pepper
200g (7oz) peeled shrimps
1 large can mussels
1 can asparagus chunks
fresh dill
5–10 × 15ml tbsp (5–10tbsp)
*   mayonnaise*
½ lemon
salt
paprika
a pinch of cayenne

1 Boil beans until barely tender in lightly salted water, drain and cool in a colander. Hard-boil the eggs, remove shells and cut into wedges.
2 Wash cucumber and tomatoes and cut into pieces and wedges. Sprinkle them with a pinch of salt. Cut pepper into narrow strips.
3 Mix together a salad sauce of mayonnaise and lemon juice and some of the juices from mussels and shrimps. Season with salt, paprika and pinch of cayenne. Drain mussels, shrimps and asparagus.
Mix all ingredients in a bowl and garnish with fresh dill. Serve well chilled with toast or French bread.

Chicory Salad with Shrimps
(serves 4)
Preparation time: about 15 min

2 heads of chicory
½ lemon
2–3 shallots or button onions
1 small red pepper
4 ripe tomatoes
fresh dill
about 100–200g (4–7oz) peeled
*   shrimps*
200ml (7fl oz) plain yoghurt
2 × 15ml tbsp (2tbsp) tomato purée
lemon juice
salt, pepper
1 small clove of garlic

1 Rinse chicory quickly or dry with a damp cloth. They should never be left in water. Cut away some of the root with a pointed knife, cut leaves across the way and squeeze lemon juice over.

2 Peel onions and cut into thin rings. Wash and deseed pepper and cut into thin rings. Cut tomatoes into wedges and drain shrimps in a colander.
3 Mix all ingredients together with dill in a salad bowl. Mix together a salad sauce from yoghurt, tomato purée and lemon juice and season with salt, pepper and crushed garlic. Pour salad sauce over salad and serve well chilled with toast and butter.

· Above : Chicory Salad with Shrimps.
Right : West Coast Salad.
Both are served with salad sauce and bread and butter.

Herring Salad

(serves 4–6)
Preparation time: 15–20 min
Settling time: about 30 min

1 lettuce
2 eggs
4 herring fillets (try a mixture of
  smoked – buckling – and rollmop
  fillets)
about 100g (4oz) cooked tongue or
  ham
2 boiled potatoes
2 onions, 1 chunk of cucumber
1 sprig of parsley, finely chopped
2 × 15ml tbsp (2tbsp) finely chopped
  chives
1 × 15ml tbsp (1tbsp) white wine
  vinegar
1–2 × 5ml tsp (1–2tsp) strong
  mustard
3–4 × 15ml tbsp (3–4tbsp) oil
salt
coarsely ground black pepper

Herring Salad can be served with or
on brown bread.

1 Rinse lettuce leaves and shake dry in a cloth. Place leaves in a plastic bag in the bottom of the refrigerator. Hard-boil the eggs.
2 Soak the herring fillets and cut into pieces at an angle. Cut the tongue and potatoes into cubes.
3 Coarsely chop the onion and cut cucumber into small cubes. Mix everything, except the eggs and lettuce leaves, in a bowl.
4 Mix together a dressing of vinegar, mustard, oil, salt and pepper and finely chopped herbs. Pour dressing over salad and cover and leave in a cold place for about ½ hr before serving.
5 Coarsely chop the eggs. Place the crisp lettuce leaves on a dish, arrange herring salad on top and sprinkle with the chopped eggs.

Pepper and Tuna Salad can be served either as a first course or as part of a cold buffet.

sieve the yolks into the mustard sauce. Season sauce with salt, pepper, lemon juice and tarragon.
3 Mix some of the peas and finely chopped celery in $\frac{3}{4}$ of the mustard sauce and divide the majority of it between the peppers. Squeeze some of the oil out of the tuna, and place pieces of tuna in the peppers. Mash the rest of the fish, mix it with the remaining mustard sauce with finely chopped egg white (from the soft-boiled egg) and fill the holes in the hard-boiled egg whites.
Place the rest of the sauce with peas and celery on a dish and place stuffed peppers and eggs on top. Sprinkle with parsley. Serve with French bread or rolls.

Holiday Salad
(serves 5–6)
Preparation time: about 15 min

1 large bunch of radishes
3–4 boiled potatoes
about 225g ($\frac{1}{2}$lb) cooked green beans
2 cans of tuna fish in oil
salt, pepper
1 lemon
1 bunch of chives, finely chopped

1 Wash radishes and cut into thin slices. Cut cold potatoes into small chunks and beans into pieces. Mix all vegetables in a bowl and sprinkle with salt and pepper.
2 Drain oil from cans over the vegetables, and squeeze lemon juice on top. Cut tuna into pieces and mix into salad. Sprinkle with chives.
Serve salad freshly made with or without bread and butter.

Broccoli Salad
(serves 4–5)
Preparation time: about 10 min

250–300g (9–11oz) fresh or frozen broccoli
1 can tuna fish in oil
2–3 eggs
salt, pepper
1 × 15ml tbsp (1tbsp) tarragon vinegar
mild mustard (Dijon)
2–3 × 15ml tbsp (2–3tbsp) oil
fresh or dried tarragon

Tuna Fish Salads

Pepper and Tuna Salad
(serves 4)
Preparation time: about 20 min

2 large red peppers
3 eggs
$\frac{1}{2}$kg (1$\frac{1}{4}$lb) fresh or 250g (9oz) frozen green peas
salt and pepper
2 × 5ml tsp (2tsp) mild French mustard (Dijon)
100–150ml (4–5fl oz) olive oil
1 lemon

1 × 15ml tbsp (1tbsp) finely chopped tarragon
1 can tuna fish in oil
2 stalks celery
finely chopped parsley

1 Halve peppers lengthways and take out seeds. Hard-boil 2 eggs and soft-boil the other. Bring fresh peas just to the boil in lightly salted water or thaw frozen ones in a sieve.
2 Carefully remove the yolk from the soft-boiled egg (*don't* take any of the white) and mix with the mustard. Add oil in drops, as with mayonnaise and stir continually. Halve the hard-boiled eggs, and

Tuna Fish in Cucumber is nice and light.

1 Rinse fresh broccoli well, cut into pieces and boil in lightly salted water for about 5 min. Frozen broccoli should be boiled in lightly salted water for 1 min.

2 Place pieces of tuna on a flat dish and place broccoli on top. Boil the eggs (4–6 min), cut into wedges and place on salad. Sprinkle with a pinch of salt and pepper.

3 Mix a dressing of vinegar, mustard to taste, salt, pepper and oil and sprinkle over salad. Sprinkle finely chopped fresh tarragon on top. Serve with French bread.

Tuna Fish in Cucumber
(serves 4–6)
Preparation time: about 15 min
Settling time: about 30 min

1 large, thick cucumber
salt
1 can tuna fish in oil
1 lemon
50g (2oz) butter
pepper
2 hard-boiled eggs
about 225g (½lb) long-grain rice,
  cooked
about 200g (10z) sweetcorn
  (canned)
1–2 × 15ml tbsp (1–2tbsp) white
  wine vinegar
3–5 × 15ml tbsp (3–5tbsp) oil

1 Wash cucumber, cut into 4 pieces, and slice lengthways. Scrape out pips and sprinkle with coarse salt. Place with cut facing down in a colander.

2 Set aside 2 × 15ml tbsp (2tbsp) boiled rice. Mix the rest of the rice with drained sweetcorn, cover the bottom of a large plate, and sprinkle with an oil/vinegar dressing seasoned with salt and pepper. Leave dish in a cold place for about ½ hr.

3 Drain most of the oil from the tuna, and mash until soft, with soft butter and lemon juice. Mix in finely chopped eggs and the 2tbsp rice and season with salt and pepper. Dry the cucumber pieces, fill with tuna mixture, and place on top of the corn/rice mixture.
Serve with white bread or brown bread.

Tuna and Grapefruit Salad
(serves 4)
Preparation time: about 15 min

2 grapefruit
1 can tuna fish in oil
1 thin leek
2 × 15ml tbsp (2tbsp) corn
  or soya oil
3–4 × 15ml tbsp (3–4tbsp)
  mayonnaise
3–4 × 15ml tbsp (3–4tbsp) plain
  yoghurt
1 lemon
salt, pepper
2 small tomatoes
fresh dill

1 Slice the grapefruit in half and remove flesh in pieces (without membranes). Clean the grapefruit shell.

2 Flake well-drained tuna. Peel and clean leek and cut into paper-thin rings.

3 Mix a salad sauce of mayonnaise, yoghurt, lemon juice, salt and pepper to taste. Mix tuna, grapefruit pieces and leek rings together, and divide mixture between grapefruit shells. Pour some sauce over each salad.

4 Garnish with small tomato wedges and fresh sprigs of dill. Serve with rolls.

Salads with Eggs and Cheese

termilk or sour cream, mayonnaise and lemon juice and season with finely chopped onion, crushed garlic and finely chopped herbs.

3 Cut radishes into thin slices and mix with the potato cubes into the salad sauce. Leave in a cold place.

Hard-boil the eggs, remove shells and cool completely. Season salad with more salt if necessary. Place halved eggs on top and garnish with herbs.

Serve cold with dishes of fried or smoked fish.

Blue Cheese Salad (left)
(serves 4)
Preparation time: 10 min

1 iceberg or any crisp lettuce
2–3 tomatoes
about 200g (7oz) blue cheese
100ml (4fl oz) buttermilk or sour
  cream
1–2 × 15ml tbsp (1–2tbsp)
  mayonnaise
1 garlic clove or 1 onion

1 Rinse or dry lettuce with a damp cloth, and shred. Cut washed tomatoes into slices and sprinkle with a pinch of salt. Cut about 150g (5 oz) cheese into small cubes with a thin, sharp knife.

2 Place lettuce, cheese and tomato lightly in a bowl and leave in a cold place.

3 Mash the rest of the cheese well and stir in buttermilk or sour cream and mayonnaise. Season sauce with crushed garlic or finely chopped onion and sprinkle over lettuce, tomatoes and cheese.

Serve freshly made with toast or salty biscuits.

Potato Salad with Radishes and Eggs (right)
(serves 4)
Preparation time: about 15 min
Settling time: ½–1 hr

6–8 firm potatoes
about 300ml (½pt) buttermilk or sour
  cream
3–4 × 15ml tbsp (3–4tbsp)
  mayonnaise
2 shallots or small onions
salt, pepper
1 garlic clove
½ lemon
about 4 × 15ml tbsp (4tbsp) finely
  chopped herbs (dill, parsley,
  chives)
1 bunch of radishes
2–4 eggs

1 Boil potatoes in their skins and peel them. Allow to get completely cold. Cut potatoes into thin slices or small cubes.

2 Mix together a salad sauce of but-

Fennel and Cheese Salad

(serves 4–6)
Preparation time: about 15 min
Setting time: 5–10 min

1 fennel bulb
a few celery stalks
½ red pepper
½ green pepper
1 bunch of radishes
150–200g (5–7oz) Gruyère or
    Emmenthal cheese
1 lettuce
cress
fresh, green herbs
about 100ml (4fl oz) Red Wine
    Dressing (see page 9)

1 Rinse fennel and celery well.
Finely chop the celery and cut the
fennel into thin slices, then into thin
strips. Clean peppers and cut into
thin strips.
2 Wash and top and tail radishes
and slice. Cut cheese into cubes.
Rinse lettuce leaves and shake off
excess water.
3 Mix everything in a salad bowl
and pour wine dressing over. Leave
in a cold place for 5–10 min.
Garnish with finely chopped cress
and other green herbs before
serving.
Serve salad with bread or rolls and
butter.

Egg Salad with Sour Cream Sauce

(serves 4)
Preparation time: about 10 min

½–1 iceberg lettuce or Chinese
    cabbage
4 eggs
½–1 lemon
200ml (7fl oz) sour cream
1 × 5ml tsp (1tsp) white wine
    vinegar
1 × 15ml tbsp (1tbsp) chives
salt, pepper

1 Rinse lettuce leaves and shake off
excess water. If the lettuce is firm,

Left: Gruyère or Emmenthal cheese and fennel make an exciting combination.

remove the outer leaves and coarsely chop it all up. Hard-boil eggs, remove shells and slice.

2 Place lettuce on a dish and sprinkle with a little lemon juice. Mix in eggs and season with salt and freshly ground pepper.

3 Mix together a sauce of sour cream, wine vinegar and remaining lemon juice. Season with finely chopped chives, salt and pepper. Pour sour cream sauce over salad. Serve freshly made with bread.

Bean Salad with Cheese
(serves 4)
Preparation time: about 15 min
Settling time: about 1 hr

½kg (1¼lb) frozen green beans
2 shallots or small onions
100–200g (4–7oz) mushrooms

about 200g (7oz) Cheddar or
*   Gruyère cheese*
1–2 lemons
salt, pepper
4 × 15ml tbsp (4tbsp) oil
4 × 15ml tbsp (4tbsp) finely chopped
*   herbs (parsley, savory, dill etc)*

1 Boil beans until barely tender in lightly salted water. Pour off water and place beans in a bowl with thin onion rings. Toss together a dressing of about half the juice of the lemons, salt, pepper and oil. Pour dressing over the warm beans and put bowl in a cool place.

2 Clean mushrooms and slice, and sprinkle with the remaining lemon juice, to avoid discoloration. Cut cheese into fairly thick slices, and then into strips.

3 Mix mushroom slices and cheese strips with the cold beans and leave salad to settle for 15–20 min. Sprinkle with finely chopped herbs. Serve chilled with wholemeal bread and butter.

Egg Salad for Sandwiches
(serves 4)
Preparation time: about 10 min

2–3 eggs
1 punnet of cress
100g (4oz) mayonnaise
2 × 5ml tsp (2tsp) curry powder
½ × 5ml tsp (½tsp) turmeric
lemon juice
single cream
salt, pepper

1 Hard-boil the eggs and cool in cold water. Remove shells and chop coarsely.

2 Mix together mayonnaise, curry powder and turmeric, and add a little cream, until the sauce has a nice firm consistency, not too thin. Season with lemon juice, salt and pepper.
Add chopped eggs and finely chopped cress and mix carefully.
Serve salad on toast or between slices of brown bread. The egg salad is also suitable for any cold buffet.

Below: Egg Salad with Sour Cream Sauce is simple and tasty.

Egg and Mushroom Salad

(serves 4)
Preparation time: 10–15 min

250g (9oz) mushrooms
1 lemon
salt, pepper
2 × 15ml tbsp (2tbsp) oil
1 small onion
1 sprig of parsley
4 ripe tomatoes
2–3 eggs

1 Mix a dressing of lemon juice, salt, pepper, oil, finely chopped onion and chopped parsley. Clean mushrooms, slice, and place in dressing immediately.
2 Wash tomatoes, cut into four wedges and sprinkle with a pinch of salt. Hard-boil eggs, remove shell and cut in slices.
3 Arrange mushroom salad in the middle of a dish and place tomato wedges and egg slices around it. Garnish with small sprigs of parsley.

Summer Salad

(serves 4)
Preparation time: 10–15 min

1 grapefruit
1 orange
1 small avocado pear
3–4 ripe tomatoes
1 lettuce
about 200g (7oz) cottage cheese
salt, pepper
3 × 15ml tbsp (3tbsp) grated, mild
  Cheddar cheese
2 × 5ml tsp (2tsp) mild mustard
1 × 15ml tbsp (1tbsp) white wine
  vinegar
2 × 15ml tbsp (2tbsp) tomato purée
1 × 15ml tbsp (1tbsp) oil

1 Peel grapefruit and orange, remove all membranes from each segment, and cut into pieces.
2 Cut avocado in two and remove the stone. Peel avocado and cut meat into thin slices. Rinse lettuce leaves and shake off excess water. Wash tomatoes and cut into wedges.
3 Place lettuce leaves on a dish and place grapefruit, orange, avocado and tomatoes over. Season cottage cheese to taste with salt and pepper and place in a heap in the middle.
4 Sprinkle grated cheese over salad and a dressing made of mustard, vinegar, tomato purée, oil, salt and pepper.

Tomatoes with Carrot Salad

(serves 4)
Preparation time: 10–15 min

4–6 large ripe tomatoes
4 carrots
1 stalk celery
3–4 × 15ml tbsp (3–4tbsp) sour
  cream
50g (2oz) cream cheese
salt, pepper
lemon juice

1 Wash tomatoes, cut off a lid and remove the insides. Peel carrots, and coarsely grate them. Clean celery, and chop up very finely. Mix the flesh and seeds of tomatoes with celery and carrots, sour cream, cream cheese, lemon juice and spices to taste. Put mixture in a cold place for about 40 min.
2 Sprinkle the scooped-out tomatoes with salt and leave to stand for about 20 mins.
3 Fill tomatoes with salad and serve at once.
French bread goes well with this dish.

Chef's Salad

(serves 4–6)
Preparation time: 10–15 min

1 iceberg or crisp lettuce
4 tomatoes
½ cucumber
150g (5oz) cooked ham
150g (5oz) mild Cheddar cheese
watercress or cress
For the Pink Salad Sauce:
100g (4oz) mayonnaise
100ml (4fl oz) mild chili sauce
1 × 15ml tbsp (1tbsp) tomato purée
salt, pepper
lemon juice

1 Rinse lettuce, cut into strips, and place on a tray. Cut tomatoes into wedges and cucumber into thin slices. Cut ham and cheese into strips.
2 Place everything in groups on top of lettuce and garnish with small clusters of cress. Mix together a salad sauce of mayonnaise and the mild chili sauce. Season with tomato purée, salt, pepper and lemon juice. Serve salad with sauce and toast.

Above: Egg and Mushroom Salad.
Centre: Summer Salad.
Below: Tomatoes with Carrot Salad.

Meat Salads

There is a huge variety of ingredients to choose from when making salads. Cold meats make substantial and delicious salads which can be served as a main course for a lunch or supper all year round.

Bacon and Egg Salad
(serves 4–6)
Preparation time: 10–15 min
Settling time: 15–20 min

700–900g (1½–2lb) firm, boiled
  potatoes
about 150g (5oz) thin bacon rashers
4 eggs
1 bunch of radishes
10–12 small, black olives
finely chopped parsley, chives
½ portion Herb Dressing (see page 9)

1 Cut cold, peeled potatoes into cubes or slices. Sprinkle with the herb dressing and leave for 15–20 min. Cut thin bacon into pieces, and fry until crisp.
2 Boil eggs for 7–8 min, peel them

and cut into thin slices. Wash, top and tail radishes and slice.
3 Mix potatoes, bacon, radishes, eggs and olives in a large salad bowl and sprinkle with parsley and chives.
Serve with brown bread and butter.

Chicken Salad with Grapefruit
(serves 4–6)
Preparation time: about 15 min
Cooking time: about 20 min

100g (4oz) long grain rice
about 250g (9oz) green beans
2 × 15ml tbsp (2tbsp) oil
2 grapefruit
salt, pepper
½ cooked chicken
parsley or cress

1 Put rice into 300ml (½pt) boiling water with ½ × 5ml tsp (½tsp) salt added and boil, covered, for 20 min on low heat. At the same time boil beans until barely tender in lightly salted water.
2 Peel grapefruit, divide into segments, and pull off as much membrane as possible. Cut segments into pieces on a plate, and mix with oil, salt and pepper to taste.

Sprinkle this dressing over warm, well drained beans and rice and leave to cool.

3 Take chicken off the bones, skin and cut into slices or cubes. Mix chicken, rice, beans and grapefruit together. Sprinkle finely chopped parsley or cress on top.

Serve with slices of white bread, fried in butter until crisp and golden.

Vegetable Salad with Ham

(serves 4–6)
Preparation time: 15–20 min
Cooking time: 6–8 min

300–400g (11–14oz) Brussels
  sprouts
250g (9oz) fresh mushrooms
1 red pepper
150–200g (5–7oz) cooked ham
4 slices of crustless white bread
25g (1oz) butter
1 × 15ml tbsp (1tbsp) oil
2 × 15ml tbsp (2tbsp) grated cheese
1 clove of garlic
½ portion Green Salad Sauce (page 6)

1 Wash and prepare Brussels sprouts. Boil until just tender in

From left : Vegetable Salad with Ham, Chicken Salad with Grapefruit, and Bacon and Egg Salad.

lightly salted water. Pour off water and cut each sprout in two.

2 Cut off the mushroom stalks and clean separately under cold, running water. Drain in a sieve or colander (*never* leave mushrooms in water). Then slice.

3 Wash and deseed pepper. Cut into cubes and mix with sprouts, mushrooms and ham cubes.

4 Cut bread into cubes and sauté until lightly golden in butter and oil. Sprinkle with grated cheese and crushed garlic. Mix bread cubes in to the salad just before serving.

Serve with a dollop of Green Salad Sauce.

Chicken or Turkey Salad

(serves 4)
Preparation time: about 15 min

6 small tomatoes
½ cucumber
2–3 red apples
1 lemon
chicken or turkey breast meat
100g (4oz) mayonnaise
1 × 15ml tbsp (1 tbsp) tarragon
    vinegar
salt, pepper
fresh or dried tarragon

1 Cut tomatoes into small wedges and cucumber into thin, halved slices. Wash apples and cut into cubes (leave the peel on). Sprinkle apples with lemon juice.
2 Cut chicken or turkey meat into thin slices and mix into salad.
3 Mix mayonnaise with vinegar, salt, pepper and tarragon to taste.

VARIATION
The salad can also be made with fresh or canned pears, cut into cubes (or lightly boiled celeriac cubes) instead of apples. Season sauce with dill instead of tarragon.

Chicken Salad with Ham and Cheese

(serves 4)
Preparation time: about 15 min

1 lettuce
½ lemon
6–8 small, ripe tomatoes
50–100g (2–4oz) cooked ham
100–150g (4–5oz) mild cheese
    (Gruyère or Emmenthal)
chicken breast meat
100g (4oz) mayonnaise
2 × 5ml tsp (2tsp) mild mustard
1 × 15ml tbsp (1 tbsp) cream
salt, pepper

1 Wash lettuce and shake until dry. Place lettuce leaves on a dish.
2 Scald and peel tomatoes and slice. Sprinkle with a little salt and lemon juice. Slice ham and cheese and chicken into strips. Mix everything and place on lettuce leaves.
3 Season mayonnaise with mustard, cream, salt and pepper.

The chicken salads (on the left and top above) can be made with cold turkey as well. Right below: Chicken Salad with Ham and Cheese.

Swiss Ham Salad (left); Ham Salad with Yoghurt Sauce (right above); and Spring Ham Salad (right below).

Spring Ham Salad

(serves 4)
Preparation time: 15–20 min

1 lettuce
1 bunch of radishes
½ cucumber
150g (5oz) cooked ham
100g (4oz) mild cheese (Cheddar or Gruyère)
1 × 15ml tbsp (1tbsp) white wine vinegar
4–5 × 15ml tbsp (4–5tbsp) olive oil
salt, pepper
1 clove of garlic

1 Rinse lettuce and shake off excess water.
2 Slice radishes and cucumber thinly and cut cucumber across. Sprinkle with salt. Cut ham and cheese into thin strips and mix everything together.
3 Make a dressing of vinegar, spices, crushed garlic and oil and sprinkle over salad.

Ham Salad with Yoghurt Sauce

(serves 4)
Preparation time: about 10 min

½ iceberg lettuce or Chinese cabbage
1 onion
100–150g (4–5oz) cooked ham
3–4 × 15ml tbsp (3–4tbsp) plain yoghurt
1 × 5ml tsp (1tsp) white wine vinegar
1–2 × 5ml tsp (1–2tsp) strong mustard

Swiss Ham Salad

(serves 6)
Preparation time: about 15 min

1 lettuce
6 ripe tomatoes
250g (9oz) cooked ham
left-over meat from a chicken or turkey
200g (7oz) Gruyère or Emmenthal cheese
200g (7oz) mayonnaise
2–3 × 15ml tbsp (2–3tbsp) double cream
½ lemon
mild mustard
salt, white pepper
cress or other green herbs

1 Pull lettuce leaves apart, rinse and shake off excess water. Divide lettuce leaves between 6 plates. Place tomato slices on top and sprinkle with salt and pepper.
2 Cut ham, chicken or turkey and cheese into thin strips and divide between the plates.
3 Mix mayonnaise, cream and lemon juice together, and season sauce with mustard, salt and pepper. Place a dollop of sauce on each plate and garnish with finely chopped cress or other herbs.
Serve immediately with the rest of the salad sauce in a dish.
This salad makes a filling meal when served with French bread or rolls.

salt, pepper
1 sprig fresh dill

1 Pull lettuce leaves apart, rinse and shake off excess water. Cut leaves into large pieces.
2 Cut ham into cubes and the peeled onion into rings and mix this with the lettuce in a bowl.
3 Mix yoghurt with the vinegar and season with mustard, salt, pepper and finely chopped dill. Pour salad sauce over salad. Both iceberg lettuce and Chinese cabbage are crisp enough to be left safely in a cold place for a while. Pour sauce over salad, about $\frac{1}{2}$ hr before serving. Serve salad with bread.

Salads from Left-overs

If you ever have any suitable left-overs which are difficult to use in another way, make a salad!

Cauliflower Salad with Chicken
(serves 4–5)
Preparation time: about 15 min

1 large cauliflower
2 stalks of celery
50–75g (2–3oz) fresh or frozen peas
200ml (7fl oz) sour cream
about 100 ml (4fl oz) plain yoghurt
curry powder
salt
white pepper
lemon juice
cress
left-over cooked chicken

1 Divide cauliflower into small florets, wash well and drain in a colander. Cut celery into thin strips, and pull off threads (if any). Defrost frozen peas in a colander.
2 Mix together a salad sauce of sour cream and plain yoghurt, and add curry powder, salt, pepper and lemon juice. Mix vegetables with sauce and leave in a cold place for about ½ hr. Season.
3 Cut chicken meat into thin strips or fine, small slices. Arrange salad on small plates, sprinkle with finely chopped cress and place chicken meat on the side.
Serve with thin slices of white bread.

Left : Sausage Salad with Apples.

Right : Meat Salad.

Autumn Salad with Rice
(serves 4–5)
Preparation time: 15–20 min

6 rashers lean bacon
1 small iceberg or crisp lettuce
2 onions
2 thin leeks
¼ cucumber or 2 pickled gherkins
1 bunch of radishes
100g (4oz) boiled, long-grain rice
2 × 15ml tbsp (2tbsp) white wine vinegar
salt, pepper
6 × 15ml tbsp (6 tbsp) oil

1 Fry bacon without adding fat and drain on paper towels.

2 Rinse lettuce leaves and shake off excess water. Peel onions and leeks and cut into thin slices. Cut cucumber lengthways and then slice, or cube pickled gherkins. Wash radishes and cut into thin slices.

3 Cut bacon into bits and mix with vegetables and cold, boiled rice. Season and sprinkle with oil/vinegar dressing.

Serve with brown bread.

Sausage Salad with Apples
(serves 4)
Preparation time: about 10 min

½ Chinese cabbage
2 sour apples
1 lemon
150–200g (5–7oz) smoked boiled sausage
3 × 15ml tbsp (3tbsp) oil
2 × 15ml tbsp (2tbsp) tomato purée
salt, pepper, paprika

1 Rinse lettuce leaves, shake off excess water, and shred leaves roughly.

2 Wash apples, remove core and slice apples thinly. Sprinkle the juice of ½ lemon over to prevent them discolouring. Cut sausage into thin slices and mix with salad and apples.

3 Mix oil with tomato purée and the rest of the lemon juice and season. Pour the dressing over the salad.

Serve salad with brown bread, either for lunch or supper.

Meat Salad
(serves 4–5)
Preparation time: 15–20 min

about 300g (11oz) left-over cooked beef
2 onions
1 pepper
4 ripe tomatoes
2 pickled gherkins
about 100 ml (4fl oz) plain yoghurt
1 × 15ml tbsp (1tbsp) tomato purée
1 × 5ml tsp (1tsp) white wine vinegar
½–1 × 5ml tsp (½–1tsp) Worcestershire sauce
salt, pepper
paprika
2 × 15ml tbsp (2tbsp) finely chopped chives

1 Remove any fat from meat and cut into thin strips. Peel onions and pepper and cut into thin strips.

2 Wash tomatoes and cut into thin wedges. Mix everything in a bowl.

3 Mix a salad sauce with yoghurt, tomato purée and vinegar and season with Worcestershire sauce, salt, pepper and paprika. Pour sauce over salad and sprinkle with finely chopped chives.

Serve with bread and butter.

Bacon Salads

Green Salad with Fried Bacon
(serves 4)
Preparation time: about 15 min
Cooking time: about 15 min

1 big lettuce (iceberg, Webbs or
*   endive)*
1 lemon
salt, pepper
about 150g (5oz) raw gammon or
*   bacon in the piece*
about 100ml (4fl oz) sour cream

1 Rinse lettuce leaves, shake off excess water and shred the biggest leaves into pieces. Place in a salad bowl. Squeeze lemon on top.
2 Cut gammon or bacon into strips and fry until nicely golden in a dry frying pan. Pour off fat and add sour cream. Stir until sour cream is boiling, season with a touch of salt and pepper and pour meat and sour cream source over the lettuce leaves. Serve freshly made with brown bread and a bowl of sour cream.

Mushroom Salad with Bacon
(serves 4)
Preparation time: about 15 min

250g (9oz) mushrooms
1 lemon
1 iceberg or other crisp lettuce
1 green pepper
100–150g (4–5oz) bacon rashers
1 × 15ml tbsp (1tbsp) white wine
*   vinegar*
1 clove of garlic
salt, pepper
4 × 15ml tbsp (4tbsp) oil

1 Cut off the stalks of the mushrooms and rinse them individually under running water. Drain at once in a colander. Slice mushrooms thinly and turn in lemon juice.
2 Rinse lettuce leaves, shake off excess water and dry by shaking in a cloth. Shred. Wash, deseed, and cut pepper into thin strips.
3 Fry bacon until crisp, drain on paper towels, and crush coarsely. Mix mushrooms, pepper, lettuce and bacon lightly together and place in a salad bowl. Shake together a dressing from vinegar, crushed garlic, salt, pepper and oil, and sprinkle over the salad.
Serve with rolls or toast.

Left: Green Salad with Fried Bacon makes a filling and tasty salad.

Above: Serve Mushroom Salad with Bacon for a crisp and crunchy treat.

Asparagus Salad with Bacon
(serves 4)
Preparation time: about 20 min
Cooking time: about 20 min (for fresh asparagus)

½kg (1¼lb) fresh asparagus or 1 large
*   can of asparagus*
about 225g (½lb) fresh spinach leaves
*   (or young dandelion leaves if you*
*   live in the country)*
100–150g (4–5oz) bacon
1 lemon
2 shallots or small onions
salt, pepper
3–4 × 15ml tbsp (3–4tbsp) oil

1 Peel thick, white asparagus well and cut off the coarse part at the bottom. Boil in lightly salted water until tender, then cut into thin slices and place in a salad bowl. Squeeze juice from ½ lemon over slices. Slice canned asparagus if used.
2 Rinse spinach (or dandelion) well, and shake off water in a lettuce basket or a cloth. Cut bacon into strips, fry until golden and drain.
3 Mix the green leaves with bacon and asparagus and sprinkle with a dressing of lemon juice, grated onion, salt, pepper and oil. Serve with crisp French bread or toast.

Red Winter Cabbage Salad
(serves 5–6)
Preparation time: about 15 min

about 300g (11oz) red cabbage
about 200g (7oz) white cabbage
6–8 Brussels sprouts
2 heads chicory (optional)
1 whole fennel or 1 head of celery
2 × 15ml tbsp (2tbsp) red wine
  vinegar
salt, pepper
1 onion
6–8 × 15ml tbsp (6–8tbsp) oil
cress

1 Wash the cabbages and sprouts and slice finely. Remove dead leaves on chicory and remove some of the root with a pointed knife and shred the rest finely.
2 Wash fennel or celery and cut stalks. Coarsely grate the fennel root or cut into fine strips.
3 Mix all the vegetable ingredients together in a salad bowl and sprinkle with a dressing of vinegar, spices, grated onion and oil. Sprinkle with finely chopped cress and serve salad with fried or grilled meat.

Beetroot Salad
(serves 5–6)
Preparation: about 10 min
Settling: 20–30 min

6–8 whole, medium-sized cooked
  beetroot
2 firm, red apples
200ml (7fl oz) sour cream
½–1 lemon
1–2 × 15ml tbsp (1–2tbsp) grated
  horseradish

1 Cut beetroot into small cubes. Wash apples, remove cores, but do not peel, and cut into cubes. Mix apples and beetroot together.
2 Mix together sour cream and lemon juice and finely grated horseradish to taste. Add sour cream to salad and leave in a cold place for about ½ hr before serving.
Serve Beetroot Salad as an accompaniment to cured ham or fried pork.

Red Salads

Red Cabbage Salad
(serves 5–6)
Preparation time: about 15 min
Settling time: 1 hr

1½ × 15ml tbsp (1½tbsp) red wine
  vinegar
salt, pepper, dried rosemary
3–4 × 15ml tbsp (3–4tbsp) oil
200–300g (7–11oz) red cabbage
1–2 heads of chicory
2 stalks of celery or ½ bulb celeriac
2–3 sour apples
½ lemon
1 cucumber
finely chopped parsley

1 Mix together a dressing of wine vinegar, salt, pepper, rosemary and oil. Leave to settle for about 1 hr.
2 Finely slice cabbage. Remove dead leaves, if any, and cut away some of the root with a pointed knife. Cut away some of the chicory root, and slice into strips.
3 Wash the celery, pull off tough strings if any, and slice finely. (Or peel and coarsely grate celeriac and turn in lemon juice.) Coarsely grate apples directly into lemon juice and cut cucumber into thin half slices.
4 Mix all ingredients and sprinkle with finely chopped parsley. Pour dressing into a small bottle and serve with the salad. This salad goes particularly well with dishes containing fried pork.

Left: Red Cabbage Salad.
Top right: Beetroot Salad.
Right: Potato Salad with Beetroot.

Potato Salad with Beetroot

(serves 4–6)
Preparation time: about 10 min
Cooking time: 30 min + cooling

6–8 firm, boiled potatoes
3–4 raw beetroot
2 × 15ml tbsp (2tbsp) red wine
vinegar
salt, pepper
5–6 × 15ml tbsp (5–6tbsp) oil
3 red onions
parsley
200ml (7fl oz) sour cream
about 100ml (4fl oz) double cream

1 Rinse beetroot and place un-peeled in boiling water. Boil on low heat for 30 min. Rinse under cold, running water and place to cool in cold water. Rub peel off and cut beetroot into small cubes.

2 Cut cold potatoes into small cubes and place them in oil/vinegar dressing with salt and pepper. Peel onion and slice into rings or coarsely chop them. Stir together a salad sauce of sour cream and lightly whipped cream.

3 Pour sauce out over the bottom of a flat dish and place potatoes, onions and beetroot in stripes on top (see picture). Sprinkle with 3–4 × 15ml tbsp (3–4tbsp) finely chopped parsley.

Serve with fried or grilled meat or sausages.

Tomato and Cucumber Salads

Classic Tomato Salad (right)
(serves 4–6)
Preparation time: about 15 min
Settling time: 10–15 min

¾kg (1¼lb) ripe tomatoes
2–3 red onions
1 bunch of chives or 1 spring onion
*   with the green top*
2 × 15ml tbsp (2tbsp) red wine
*   vinegar*
salt, black pepper
5–6 × 15ml tbsp (5–6tbsp) oil
1–2 cloves of garlic

1 Wash tomatoes and cut into slices.
Clean and finely chop the onion and
the chives. Place tomato slices over-

lapping in a flat dish and sprinkle with onion and chives between and over the tomatoes.

2 Mix together vinegar, salt, pepper, oil and crushed garlic and sprinkle over salad. Leave in a cold place for 10–15 min.
Serve with any fried meat or poultry.

French Cucumber Salad (left)
(serves 4)
Preparation time: about 10 min

1 cucumber
200ml (7fl oz) sour cream
1 × 15ml tbsp (1tbsp) white wine or
*   1 × 5ml tsp (1tsp) white wine*
*   vinegar*
salt, white pepper
fresh dill

1 Wash cucumber and cut into thin slices with a cheese slicer or a very sharp knife. Place slices in a bowl.
2 Mix together a salad sauce from sour cream and white wine or wine vinegar. Season with salt, white pepper, and finely chopped dill. Pour salad sauce over cucumber slices. Serve with fried chicken, meat or fish.

Tomato Salad with
Cream Sauce (right)
(serves 4)
Preparation time: about 10 min

4–6 ripe tomatoes
salt, pepper
100ml (4fl oz) sour cream
2 × 5ml tsp (2tsp) white wine
*   vinegar*
2 shallots or small onions
1 bunch of chives

1 Slice tomatoes and place on a dish. Sprinkle with a pinch of salt.
2 Mix together sour cream with wine vinegar, finely chopped onions and salt and pepper to taste. Pour sauce over tomatoes and sprinkle with finely chopped chives.
Serve freshly made, with fried or smoked fish.

Marinated Tomatoes
(serves 4)
Preparation time: about 10 min
Settling time: about 30 min

350g (12oz) small cherry tomatoes
2 × 15ml tbsp (2tbsp) red wine
*   vinegar*

salt, black pepper
4–5 × 15ml tbsp (4–5tbsp) oil
1 bunch chives
fresh or dried basil

1 Wash and dry ripe tomatoes. Cut in two and place on a dish with the flat side facing up.
2 Mix together a dressing of vinegar, salt, pepper and oil. Sprinkle over tomatoes and place dish in a cold place under cover for about 30 min.
3 Finely chop chives and basil over tomatoes just before serving. If you use dried basil, mix into the dressing first.
Serve with cold meats, grilled meat, or poultry.

Cucumber and Tomato Salad
(serves 4–5)
Preparation time: about 10 min

8 ripe tomatoes
½ cucumber
4–5 spring onions with the green top
*   or 1 bunch of chives*
2 small onions
1 lettuce
1 lemon
salt, pepper
4 × 15ml tbsp (4tbsp) oil

1 Wash tomatoes and cucumber and peel onions. Cut tomatoes into small wedges and the cucumber and onions into thin slices. Finely chop the spring onion tops, or chives.
2 Rinse leaves of lettuce separately, shake off water and shred. Place in a salad bowl with the other salad vegetables on top.
3 Dress with lemon juice, salt, pepper and oil and sprinkle some chives or spring onion green on top. Serve with fried meat and fish.

Dandelion or Endive Salads

Green Dandelion Salad
(serves 4)
Preparation time: about 10 min

1 endive or small crisp lettuce
1 handful fresh dandelion leaves
1 lemon
salt, pepper
2–3 × 15ml tbsp (2–3tbsp) oil
lemon balm, mint or parsley

1 Rinse lettuce and dandelion leaves and fresh herbs and drain.
2 Mix together a dressing of lemon juice, salt, pepper and finely chopped herbs and sprinkle over leaves. Serve with meat and fish dishes.

Dandelion Salad with Fruit
(serves 4)
Preparation time: about 15 min

1 endive or small crisp lettuce
1 handful fresh dandelion leaves
1 orange, 1 lemon
2 apples
salt, paprika
3–4 × 15ml tbsp (3–4tbsp) oil

1 Rinse endive and dandelions.
2 Peel orange, remove any membranes, and cut into pieces. Cube unpeeled apples and mix with orange, endive and dandelion leaves.
3 Mix together lemon juice and oil and season with salt and paprika. Pour dressing over salad.
Serve freshly made with roast game.

Spring Salad (right)
(serves 4)
Preparation time: about 10 min

1 endive
1 handful fresh dandelion leaves
2 stalks of celery
50–100g (2–4oz) small, black olives
2–3 × 15ml tbsp (2–3tbsp) pine
  kernels or sesame seeds
1 lemon
salt, pepper
4 × 15ml tbsp (4tbsp) oil

1 Rinse endive and dandelion leaves and mix with finely chopped celery.
2 Sprinkle olives and pine kernels over salad with a dressing of lemon juice, salt, pepper and oil on top.
Serve freshly made with fried meat.

Above : Green Dandelion Salad.   Below : Dandelion Salad with Fruit.

Avocado Mousse with Crab
(serves 4)
Preparation time: about 15 min
Cooling time: about 1 hr

2 ripe avocados
1 lemon
salt, pepper
1 egg-white
1 can crab meat (or mussels and/or
*   shrimps)*
fresh dill

1 Peel avocados, remove stones and
cut flesh into pieces. Place avocado
pieces in the blender and squeeze
lemon juice on top. Run blender for
a moment until you have a fluffy
mousse. (You could also mash the
avocado with a fork and then whisk
until light.)
2 Whisk egg-white until white
peaks form, fold carefully into
avocado mixture and season with
salt and pepper. Cool mousse for
about 1 hr in refrigerator or for
10–15 min in the freezer.
3 Keep aside a few pieces of crab
(shrimp or mussels) and turn the
rest into the mousse.
Divide mousse between 4 small,
cold glasses or dishes, and garnish
with crab pieces and a few sprigs of
dill.
Serve as a first course with toast and
lemon wedges.

**Avocado Salad with Green
Beans**
(serves 4)
Preparation time: about 15 min

about 250g (9oz) green beans, fresh
*   or frozen*
salt, pepper
1 lemon
2 ripe avocados
1 × 15ml tbsp (1tbsp) tarragon
*   vinegar*
1 × 5ml tsp (1tsp) Dijon mustard
4–5 × 15ml tbsp (4–5tbsp) oil
fresh parsley or tarragon

1 Rinse and prepare beans and boil
for 5 min in lightly salted water.

Avocado Salads

Avocado and Watercress Salad
(serves 4)
Preparation time: about 15 min

1 large bunch of watercress
1 red pepper
1 thin leek
1 large, ripe avocado
3 × 15ml tbsp (3tbsp) lemon juice
1 clove of garlic
salt, pepper
paprika
4–5 × 15ml tbsp (4–5tbsp) oil

1 Rinse watercress, shake off excess
water and remove the thickest
stems. Wash and deseed pepper and
cut into small cubes. Clean leek and
cut into thin rings.
2 Whisk together a dressing of
lemon juice, crushed garlic, salt,
pepper, paprika and oil in salad
bowl.
3 Peel avocado, remove stone and
cube flesh straight into the salad
bowl. Add other ingredients and
mix salad. Serve with steak, cold
ham or with fried chicken.

(Cook frozen beans according to instructions on the packet.) Drain beans well in a sieve.

2 Peel avocados, and remove stones. Cut one of them into cubes and the other into slices. Squeeze lemon juice over at once, to avoid discoloration.

3 Mix beans and avocado cubes in a salad bowl and place the sliced avocado on top.

Pour over a dressing of tarragon vinegar, Dijon mustard, salt, pepper, oil and 1–2 × 15ml tbsp (1–2tbsp) finely chopped parsley or tarragon. Serve freshly made with French bread or toast.

Avocado and Pepper Salad

(serves 4)
Preparation time: about 15 min

1 lettuce
1 large, ripe avocado
1 large courgette or $\frac{1}{4}$ cucumber
1 lemon
salt, pepper
1 large, green pepper
1 × 5ml tsp (1tsp) white wine
  vinegar
4–5 × 15ml tbsp (4–5tbsp) oil

1 Separate lettuce leaves, rinse and shake off excess water. Squeeze the juice from lemon and pour into the salad bowl.

2 Peel avocado, remove stone, slice flesh and place in lemon juice. Peel courgette or cucumber and cut into fairly large cubes. Sprinkle with a pinch of salt and cover everything with lemon juice.

3 Wash pepper, deseed, and cut into narrow strips. Mix into salad.

4 Mix together a dressing of wine vinegar, a pinch of salt, pepper and oil. Pour dressing over salad and mix carefully until everything is soaked in lemon juice.

Serve as a first course or with brown or white bread and butter as a lunch dish.

Winter Salads

Carrot and Chicory Salad
(serves 5–6)
Preparation time: about 10 min

4–5 carrots
2 heads chicory
2 red apples
2 × 15ml tbsp (2tbsp) lemon juice
salt, pepper
3–4 × 15ml tbsp (3–4tbsp) oil

1 Scrape carrots and grate coarsely. Remove any dead outer leaves from chicory, cut off root end with a sharp knife and dry well with a damp cloth. Slice chicory across.
2 Wash apples, core and cut, unpeeled, into thin pieces. Mix at once with a dressing of lemon juice, salt, pepper and oil. Mix in grated carrots and chicory shreds.
Serve with fried pork, poultry or sausages.

Easy Cabbage Salad
(serves 5–6)
Preparation time: about 10 min
Settling time: about 15 min

about 200–300g (7–11oz) white
  cabbage
4–5 carrots
75g (3oz) raisins
1 lemon
1 × 5ml tsp (1tsp) clear honey
25–50g (1–2oz) hazelnuts, shelled

1 Shred cabbage finely and mix with coarsely grated carrots and raisins.
2 Mix lemon juice and honey with 1 × 15ml tbsp (1tbsp) cold water and add coarsely chopped hazelnuts. Pour this dressing over salad and mix lightly to spread dressing evenly.
Leave in a cold place for 5 min, and serve chilled with all sorts of fried pork dishes.

Clockwise from back: Spanish Tomato Salad, American Cabbage Salad, and Carrot and Chicory Salad.

American Cabbage Salad
(serves 5–6)
Preparation time: about 15 min

¼ cabbage (about 300g or 11oz)
1 chunk of cucumber
1 small fresh pineapple or 1 small
  can unsweetened pineapple chunks
75g (3oz) raisins
3 × 15ml tbsp (3tbsp) orange juice
1–2 × 15ml tbsp (1–2tbsp) lemon
  juice

1 Finely shred the cabbage and slice cucumber thinly. Peel pineapple with a sharp knife. Slice fruit in two halves lengthways, cut out root and cut flesh into small slices or cubes (retain the juice).
2 Mix cabbage, cucumber and pineapple with raisins. Mix orange and lemon juices and mix with pineapple juice. If you use canned pineapple, add 1 × 15ml tbsp (1tbsp) of the syrup. Sprinkle the juices over the salad and mix everything well. Serve as a lunch with bread or after dinner instead of dessert.

Spanish Tomato Salad
(serves 4)
Preparation time: about 10 min
Settling time: about 30 min

5–6 ripe tomatoes
1 large onion
1 head chicory
1 × 15ml tbsp (1tbsp) red wine
  vinegar
salt, pepper
paprika
3–4 × 15ml tbsp (3–4tbsp) olive oil

1 Wash tomatoes and slice. Clean and coarsely chop the onion.
2 Remove any dead outer leaves from chicory and dry the rest with a damp cloth. Cut out the root end with a pointed knife and cut the chicory into tiny, thin strips.
3 Put the tomato slices, chicory shreds and coarsely chopped onion in a deep salad bowl. Sprinkle over a dressing made with the wine vinegar, salt, pepper, paprika and oil. Leave to rest for about ½ hr.
Serve the tomato salad with roast beef or steak, or grilled or roast chicken.

Green Potato Salad is tasty and good to look at.

Green Potato Salad

(serves 4–5)
Preparation time: about 15 min
Settling time: 1–2 hr

1 kg (2¼ lb) new potatoes
2 red onions
1 sprig of dill
1 sprig of parsley
1 bunch of chives
2 × 15ml tbsp (2tbsp) wine vinegar
1 × 15ml tbsp (1tbsp) lemon juice
salt, black pepper
1 clove of garlic
6–8 × 15ml tbsp (6–8tbsp) oil

1 Boil potatoes in their skins.
2 Peel and coarsely chop onions. Finely chop the herbs, mix with onions, and add to a dressing of vinegar, lemon juice, salt, pepper, crushed garlic and oil. Shake well.
3 Rinse potatoes in cold water and peel them. Cut into slices, directly into dressing. Mix carefully so that potato slices do not break or fall apart. Turn potatoes from time to time while salad is cooling.
Serve with dishes of fried or cured meat, boiled meat, sausages, grilled meat, fish or poultry.

Cabbage and Pepper Salad
(serves 6)
Preparation time: about 10 min

¼ large or ½ smaller cabbage
2 thin leeks
1 red pepper
1 sprig of parsley
2 × 15ml tbsp (2tbsp) tarragon vinegar or other spicy vinegar
salt, black pepper
garlic salt (optional)
6 × 15ml tbsp (6tbsp) oil

1 Finely shred the cabbage. Clean leeks and slice into thin rings. Wash and deseed pepper, and slice into small strips.

2 Mix salad vegetables with finely chopped parsley and sprinkle with a dressing of spicy vinegar, salt, pepper, garlic salt (if used) and oil. Serve salad well chilled with all kinds of fried meat dishes, mince dishes, sausages etc.

NB: This is one of the very few salads which can be stored until the next day, tightly covered with plastic film in the refrigerator. Sprinkle a touch of fresh, finely chopped parsley over it before serving.

Potato Salad with Cream Sauce
(serves 6)
Preparation time: about 15 min
Settling time: about 1 hr

1.1–1.4kg (2½–3lb) small, firm, boiled potatoes
100g (4oz) mayonnaise
100–200ml (4–7fl oz) sour cream
½ lemon
a little single cream (or top of milk)

1 large onion
1 bunch of chives
salt, pepper, paprika
1 punnet of cress
3–4 small, ripe tomatoes

1 Boil potatoes in their skins, preferably the day before you make the salad. Rinse under cold, running water, peel and leave, covered, in a cold place.
2 Mix a salad sauce of mayonnaise, sour cream, lemon juice and cream or top of milk. Add finely chopped or grated onion, finely chopped chives, salt and pepper to taste and about ½ the cress.
3 Cut potatoes into slices or cubes, mix into salad sauce and leave in a cold place for about 1 hr. Season with more salt and pepper, if necessary. Put salad in a bowl and garnish with a sprinkling of paprika, tomatoes cut into wedges and small clusters of cress.
Serve with all kinds of roasted or baked meat or fish dishes.

French Pepper Salad
(serves 4)
Preparation time: about 15 min

4 firm, boiled potatoes
1 red, 1 green and 1 yellow pepper
* 10–15 black grapes*
about 100g (4oz) Feta or cottage cheese
1 × 15ml tbsp (1tbsp) red wine vinegar
salt, black pepper
3–4 × 15ml tbsp (3–4tbsp) olive oil or other good quality oil

1 Peel the cold potatoes, slice, and put in a salad bowl. Wash and deseed peppers and cut into strips.
2 Mix peppers with halved black grapes (pipped) and small pieces of Feta or cottage cheese in a bowl.
3 Shake together a dressing of vinegar, salt, coarsely ground black pepper and oil and sprinkle over salad.
Serve with French bread or other bread.

Finely shredded cabbage, peppers and leeks are good winter vegetables to use in a salad.

Colourful Salad (below)
(serves 4)
Preparation time: about 15 min

½ Webb's or iceberg lettuce
about 300g (11oz) green beans
2 eggs
2–3 tomatoes
2 stalks of celery
1 big red onion
10–12 stuffed olives
2 × 15ml tbsp (2tbsp) wine vinegar
salt, pepper
6 × 15ml tbsp (6tbsp) oil
finely chopped parsley

1 Rinse lettuce leaves, shake off excess water, and shred. Boil beans until barely tender in lightly salted water and drain in colander.
2 Hard-boil eggs and slice into wedges. Slice tomatoes and olives, cut celery into strips and red onion into thin rings.
3 Place lettuce leaves on a flat dish and arrange the other vegetables artistically on top (see photograph). Mix a dressing of vinegar, salt, pepper, oil and finely chopped parsley and sprinkle over salad.
Serve with brown bread.

Winter Salad with Brussels Sprouts (right below)
(serves 4–5)
Preparation time: about 20 min
Settling time: 20–30 min

about 250g (9oz) Brussels sprouts
1 large parsnip
3–4 carrots
1 lemon
1 red pepper
2–3 pickled gherkins
2 × 15ml tbsp (2tbsp) brine from
  gherkins
5 × 15ml tbsp (5tbsp) oil
salt, pepper
4–5 × 15ml tbsp (4–5tbsp) cottage
  cheese
finely chopped parsley

1 Wash and prepare the sprouts, and cut them in half.
2 Peel and grate the parsnip and the carrots, and dress immediately with the lemon juice.
3 Wash and deseed the pepper and cut into cubes. Cube the gherkins.
4 Mix all the salad ingredients together in a bowl, and dress with the gherkin brine, oil, salt and pepper. Chill for 20–30 min.

Place dollops of cottage cheese on top of the salad, and sprinkle with finely chopped parsley.
Serve with brown bread and butter.

Cabbage Salad with Mandarin Oranges (right)
(serves 4–5)
Preparation time: 10–15 min

200–300g (7–11oz) cabbage
2–3 sour apples
2–3 mandarin oranges (satsumas or
  tangerines)
a few white grapes
walnuts
1 × 15ml tbsp (1tbsp) oil
1 lemon

1 Finely shred the cabbage and place in a salad bowl. Wash apples, coarsely grate directly into the salad bowl, and squeeze lemon juice over. Mix salad carefully with two forks.
2 Peel mandarins (or satsumas or tangerines) and divide into segments. Mix into salad, with halved, pipped grapes and coarsely chopped walnuts. Sprinkle the oil over the salad and toss well.
Serve with fried meat.

Any salad can, of course, be served as a lunch dish, but this combination of crisp salad vegetables with 4 different sauces is particularly refreshing – as well as good to look at!

Special Lunchtime Salad
(serves 6–8)
Preparation time: about 40 min in all

2 small, green peppers
1 red pepper
1 lemon
250g (9oz) fresh button mushrooms

450g (1lb) small cherry tomatoes
½ iceberg or Webb's lettuce
about 200g (7oz) fresh or canned beansprouts
1 cucumber
2–3 red onions
3–4 spring onions with green tops or 2 onions and a handful of chives
3–4 cooked beetroots

1 Clean all vegetables and cut evenly into small slices, cubes or strips. Sprinkle mushrooms with lemon juice.

2 Place everything in strips on a dish. The salad can be left covered in the fridge for $\frac{1}{2}$–1 hr.

Serve with bread or several salad sauces.

Tomato Sauce

200–300ml (7–10fl oz) sour cream
1–2 × 15ml tbsp (1–2tbsp) tomato
purée
1 clove of garlic
lemon juice
salt, pepper
fresh or dried basil

Mix sour cream, tomato purée and crushed garlic together. Season with lemon juice, salt, pepper and basil.

Egg Yolk Sauce

4 eggs
175ml (6fl oz) oil
1–1$\frac{1}{2}$ × 15ml tbsp (1–1$\frac{1}{2}$tbsp) Dijon
mustard
1–2 × 15ml tbsp (1–2tbsp) dry
vermouth
salt, white pepper
curry powder

Hard-boil 1 egg. Boil 3 eggs for 4–6 mins. Remove shell from the 3 eggs, remove egg yolks and rub through a sieve. Add oil, a little at a time and stir until it has a smooth consistency like mayonnaise. Season with mustard, dry vermouth, salt, pepper and curry powder. Shell the hard-boiled egg, remove egg yolk and rub through a sieve onto the finished salad sauce. The egg whites can be chopped coarsely and served with the vegetables.

Avocado Sauce

2 small avocados or 1 big ripe
avocado
100g (4oz) mayonnaise
lemon juice
salt, pepper
1 clove of garlic
finely chopped parsley

Peel and cut avocado and remove stone. Cut flesh into small pieces and blend with lemon juice at a medium speed until it looks like a fine purée. (Sprinkled with lemon juice, it can also be mashed with a fork.) If avocado is very ripe, flesh can be rubbed through a nylon mesh sieve (metal sieves affect the colour of the flesh). Mix purée with mayonnaise and season with salt, pepper, crushed garlic and a further drop of lemon juice. Sprinkle sauce with finely chopped parsley or other green herb when serving.

Blue Cheese Sauce

125–150g (4$\frac{1}{2}$–5oz) Gorgonzola,
Roquefort or other blue cheese
about 100ml (4fl oz) sour cream
salt, lemon juice (optional)
25–50g (1–2oz) walnuts, shelled

Mash cheese well with a fork and stir in sour cream, a little at a time, until mixture is nice and smooth. Season with salt and lemon juice.

Coarsely chop walnuts, mix most of them in sauce and sprinkle the rest over when serving.

Salads with Fruit

Grapefruit Salad
(serves 4)
Preparation time: about 15 min

2 large or 4 small grapefruit
2 eggs
2 ripe tomatoes
8 stuffed olives
8 black olives
2 × 15ml tbsp (2tbsp) lemon juice
salt, pepper
parsley
4 × 15ml tbsp (4tbsp) oil

1 Slice large grapefruit in half or cut lid off the small grapefruit. Remove flesh in nice, small pieces and clean shells inside, removing all membrane and pith.
2 Hard-boil eggs, shell and coarsely chop. Slice tomatoes.
3 Mix grapefruit flesh, egg and tomatoes with olives and pile salad into empty grapefruit shells. Sprinkle with seasoned oil and lemon juice dressing and finely chopped parsley.
Serve well chilled as a first course or as a light supper.

Apple Salad with Grapes
(serves 4)
Preparation time: about 10 min

about 200g (7oz) black grapes
2 firm apples
1 × 15ml tbsp (1tbsp) lemon juice
2–3 × 15ml tbsp (2–3tbsp) orange juice
clear honey
a few lettuce leaves

1 Rinse grapes, slice and remove pips. Mix lemon and orange juices with clear honey in a bowl.
2 Cut apples in four, remove cores and coarsely grate straight into fruit juice, to prevent them discolouring.
3 Rinse lettuce leaves, shake off excess water and place on 4 serving dishes. Divide apples and grapes between plates. Serve as a dessert or as a salad accompanying cheese.

Left: Grapefruit Salad.
Right: Apple Salad with Grapes.

Waldorf Salad
(serves 4)
Preparation time: 10–15 min

3–4 stalks of celery or 1 small bulb celeriac
2 apples
½ lemon
50g (2oz) mayonnaise
100ml (4fl oz) double cream
25–50g (1–2oz) walnuts, shelled
a few black or white grapes

1 Wash celery, and remove any tough strips. Slice and shred finely. Peel and coarsely grate the celeriac and sprinkle with lemon juice.
2 Peel apples, cut in four and slice thinly. Sprinkle with lemon juice to prevent discoloration. Put a few half walnuts aside and coarsely chop up the rest.
3 Mix lightly whipped cream and coarsely chopped walnuts with the mayonnaise and pour salad sauce over celery and apples. Mix carefully with two forks. Put salad in a salad bowl and garnish with half walnuts and halved grapes.
Waldorf Salad goes particularly well with game, but can be served on a buffet table with cold meat.

Gardener's Salad
(serves 4–5)
Preparation time: about 15 min

2 eggs
1 lettuce
about 225g (½lb) fresh spinach leaves
1 sprig of dill
1 sprig of parsley
a few stems of fresh tarragon
1 turnip
1 red apple
1 onion
2 × 15ml tbsp (2tbsp) lemon juice
1 × 15ml tbsp (1tbsp) dry white wine
salt, black pepper
4–5 × 15ml tbsp (4–5tbsp) oil

1 Rinse lettuce and spinach leaves and shake off excess water. Hard-boil the eggs, shell and slice into wedges.
2 Peel turnip and cut it and apples into thin slices, and onion into thin rings.
3 Mix ingredients for the salad and sprinkle with a dressing of lemon juice, white wine, salt, coarsely ground pepper and oil.
Serve freshly made with brown bread.

Fennel Salad and Apple with Cheese
(serves 4)
Preparation time: about 15 min

1 whole bulb fennel with some green
  fronds on top
100g (4oz) Gruyère cheese
2 sour apples
2 shallots or small onions
50g (2oz) cream cheese
2 × 15ml tbsp (2tbsp) dry white wine
  or lemon juice
salt, pepper

Gardener's Salad – a crisp mixture of fruit and vegetables.

1 Cut root off fennel and slice the rest, including the stalks. Rinse it all well, and cut slices into thin strips.
2 Cut cheese into small cubes and coarsely chop peeled onion and peeled or unpeeled apples. Mix everything in a salad bowl.
3 Season cream cheese, mix until smooth, and then mix in the white wine or lemon juice. Pour over the salad vegetables and cheese in bowl. Garnish with frondy fennel leaves. Serve with brown bread and butter, and with any cold meat dishes.

Fruit Salad from Mallorca
(serves 4)
Preparation time: about 10 min

1 lettuce
1 orange
1 lemon
2 small, firm bananas
3–4 × 15ml tbsp (3–4tbsp) double or
    sour cream
salt
cayenne pepper

1 Rinse and dry lettuce leaves and shred. Peel the orange, and remove as much of the membranes and pith as possible. Cut flesh into pieces on a plate. Mix orange juice on plate with the juice of the lemon.
2 Peel bananas and cut into slices. Mix immediately with fruit juices to prevent discoloration. Mix lettuce leaves and fruit in a bowl.
3 Mix cream with orange and lemon juices from the bananas. Season with a pinch of salt and cayenne pepper, and pour over the salad.
Serve freshly made as lunch or dessert.

Fruit Salad from Mallorca can also
be served as a dessert.

Index